BARBARA HOLDRIDGE   *INTERNATIONAL DESIGN LIBRARY*™

AUBREY BEARDSLEY
DESIGNS · FROM · THE · AGE · OF · CHIVALRY

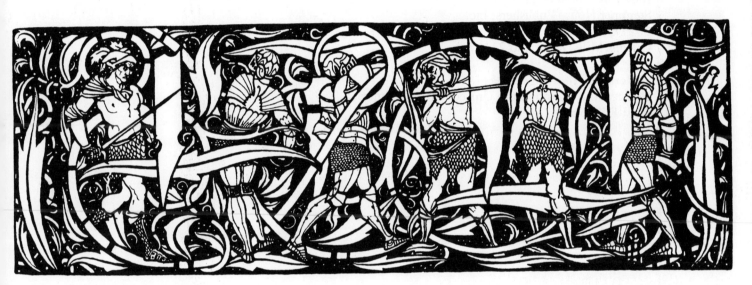

THE BIRTH LIFE AND ACTS OF KING ARTHUR OF HIS
NOBLE KNIGHTS OF THE ROUND TABLE THEIR
MARVELLOUS ENQUESTS AND ADVENTURES

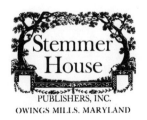

Stemmer House
PUBLISHERS, INC.
OWINGS MILLS, MARYLAND

Inquiries should be directed to
Stemmer House Publishers, Inc.
2627 Caves Road
Owings Mills, Maryland 21117

A Barbara Holdridge book
Printed and bound in the United States of America
First Edition

Introduction

UBREY BEARDSLEY lived but briefly, from 1872 to 1898; yet he did more to enrich the language of international design than perhaps any other known artist in history. Out of his inkpot flowed swirling designs, flowers and trees, seen in fevered, non-representational detail, rich fields of black, with white scintillations of bloom, gaunt and angular hags and soberly handsome damsels, evilly pure and purely evil fauns and lewd creatures. Such bold ingenuity of composition—two-dimensional planes making up designed rectangles, with their rich black-and-white borders in endless variety—had not been seen before; and they have left an indelible imprint on the art of design ever since.

Yet Beardsley was not an originator entirely; in part he was a superb synthesizer. A young disciple of Burne-Jones, he also was in the thrall of Whistler, and through Whistler, the school of Utamaro and the entire Japanese tradition of art. All of this when he was only nineteen and twenty—a poor, gangling, tubercular boy still earning his living in London by writing up insurance policies on a high stool by day, and drawing ceaselessly by night.

Through friends he did have a bit of good fortune; just recently he had presented a drawing of Richard Wagner's Siegfried to Burne-Jones, who had it hung in his drawing room. Also, he had savored a first trip to France, financed by a great-aunt's bequest. And in England he had met not only Burne-Jones, whose pseudo-medieval paintings made a deep impression on him, but Whistler, William Morris and the darling of artistic society, Oscar Wilde, who called him "a monstrous orchid."

But young Aubrey's greatest good luck—and challenge—lay before him. The story that follows is one that this publisher has cherished, as holding out hope that similar lightning can strike again, in another place and time.

Temptingly near Beardsley's place of work, in Queen Street, Cheapside, was a congenial bookshop, Jones and Evans. In 1892 Frederick Evans, the proprietor, struck up an acquaintance with the pale and gaunt boy who dipped into eighteenth-century volumes on his lunch hours; and soon (being, as so many independent booksellers still are, an interesting, artistic personage himself) started to barter a few books for drawings left with him by the lad overnight for a quick decision. One day, while looking at a sheaf of Beardsley's drawings, he recalled that another frequenter of his shop, the publisher Joseph Malaby Dent, had confided that he yearned to do an illustrated edition of the *Morte d'Arthur,* if only he could find the right artist. Acting on impulse, Evans sent a note to Dent suggesting he come over immediately, since he only had the drawings for the day. Over at once came the portly, mustachioed and bearded Dent, who, though no longer young, headed a very young publishing firm—one whose present-day incarnation, J. M. Dent & Sons Ltd., still venerates its founder through its cable address, "MALABY."

By the workings of chance, in came Beardsley as well, on his usual lunch-hour break; and much to the young clerk's astonishment, the book publisher made him the kind of offer that would have been worthy of Burne-Jones, except that he hardly wanted to pay Burne-Jones's customary fee. The money offered, however, was enough to allow Aubrey Beardsley to give notice to his employer a little while after his sample drawing was accepted by Dent. He would remain a freelance artist—mostly penurious, to be sure—to the end of his brief life.

What was this astounding commission? Nothing short of producing twenty full pages and double-page spreads, along with close to 550 initials, tail pieces, chapter headings, borders, ornaments, jacket design, title page—and even a publisher's logo for Dent—all for £250! Lucky Beardsley; lucky Dent.

If the youthful and untried artist later felt burdened by the enormous workload under pressure and turned in a somewhat uneven production, he cannot really be blamed. Taken as a whole, Beardsley's *Morte d'Arthur* is astonishing; and it had a galvanizing effect on the art world as it was published first, in sections. Beardsley worked with the line-block process suited to mass production; it dictated a minimum of fine lines and a maximum of bold effects, and this technique is as crisp, refreshing and stimulating to our eyes today as it was in 1893. Although many of the illustrations had little to do with the Arthurian dream—as satyrs and minxes do not—they had everything to do with art. Imbued with influences of Japan, Botticelli, Burne-Jones, Kelmscott medievalism and others, these designs are yet, as we realize today, uniquely, gloriously Beardsley, with their rhythms, artful repetitions, assymetrical balances, inventive borders and fantasy uses of nature motifs, all in uncompromising and visually stunning black and white. Unquestionably the portly publisher got his money's worth and his *kudos,* well deserved for taking a chance on a frail unknown; and the frail, soon-to-be consumed artist won his one-way ticket to immortality.

Modern designers and students of design will find inspiration and invention in the following pages, which include a number of illustrations enlarged and painstakingly cleaned by us, and one— a chapter heading in the medieval-illumination manner, with flower and foliage drooping beyond the right margin—that appears only in the rare third edition, limited to 1600 copies, from which we photographed the chosen designs.

B.H.

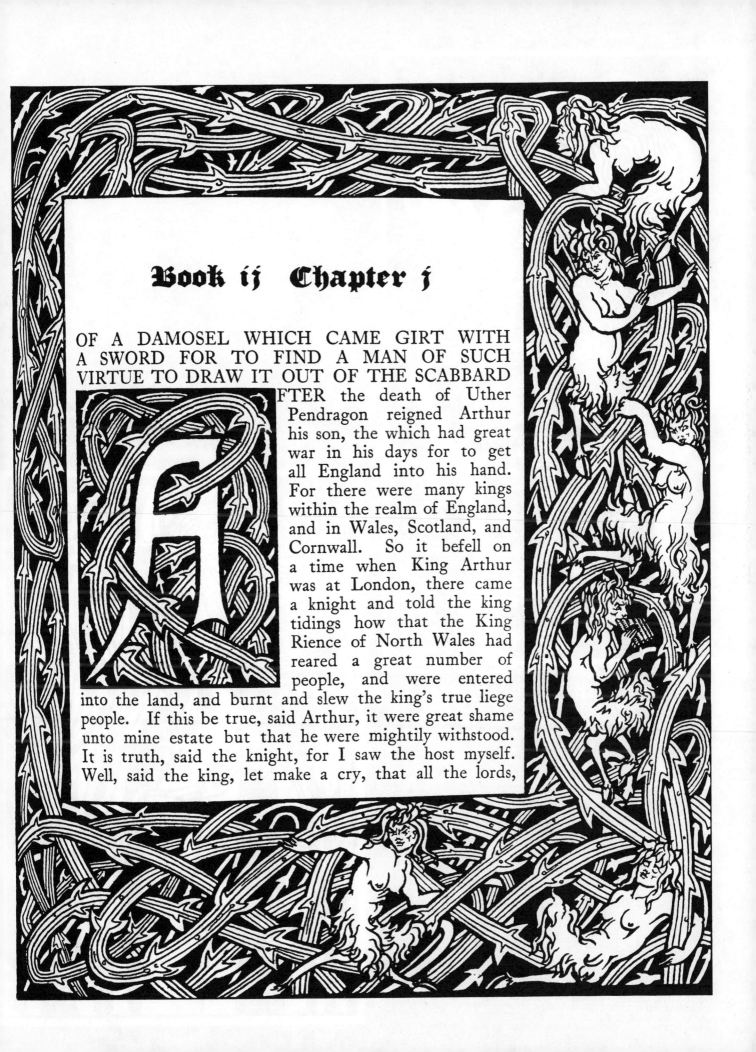

Book ij   Chapter j

OF A DAMOSEL WHICH CAME GIRT WITH
A SWORD FOR TO FIND A MAN OF SUCH
VIRTUE TO DRAW IT OUT OF THE SCABBARD

AFTER the death of Uther Pendragon reigned Arthur his son, the which had great war in his days for to get all England into his hand. For there were many kings within the realm of England, and in Wales, Scotland, and Cornwall. So it befell on a time when King Arthur was at London, there came a knight and told the king tidings how that the King Rience of North Wales had reared a great number of people, and were entered into the land, and burnt and slew the king's true liege people. If this be true, said Arthur, it were great shame unto mine estate but that he were mightily withstood. It is truth, said the knight, for I saw the host myself. Well, said the king, let make a cry, that all the lords,

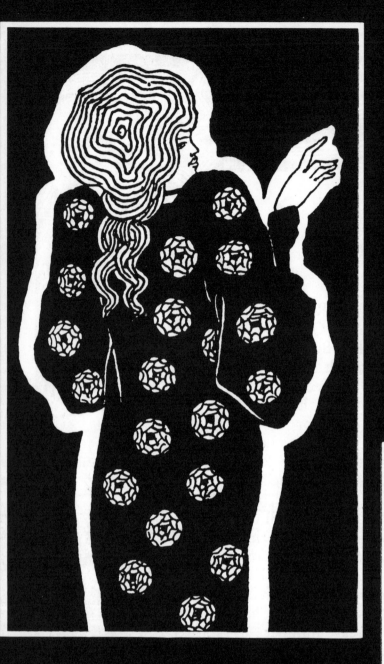

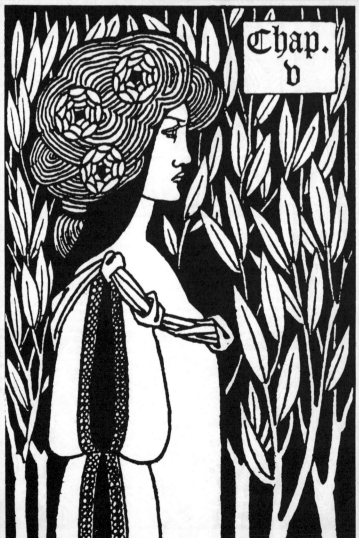

Chap. v

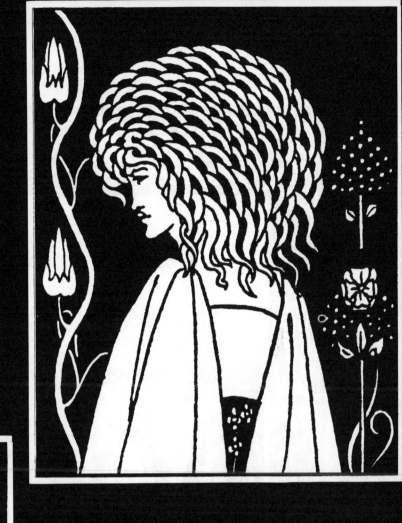
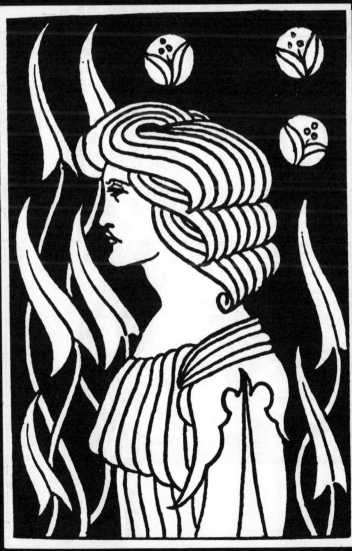

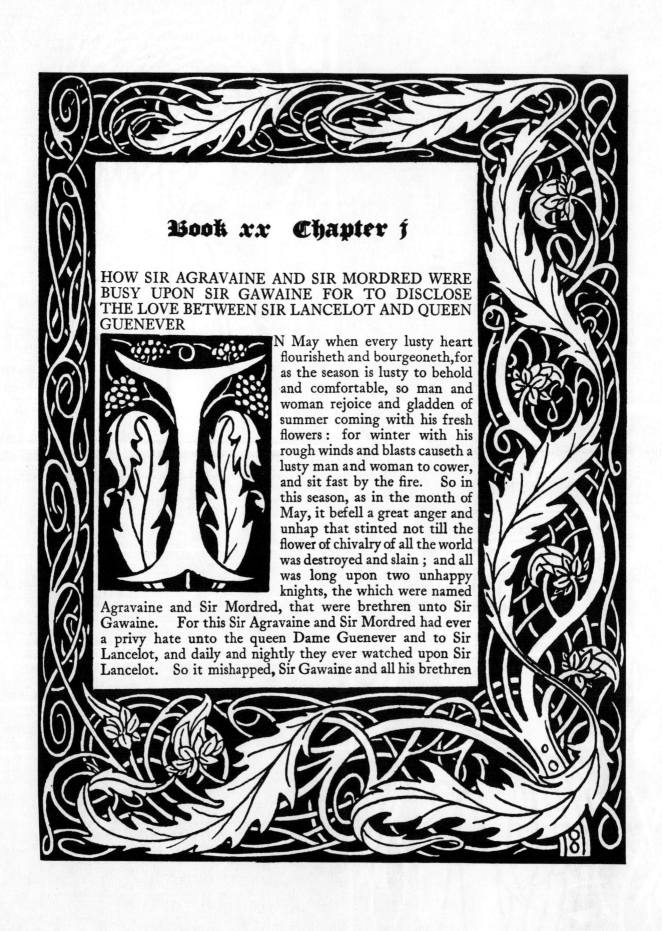

Book xx Chapter j

HOW SIR AGRAVAINE AND SIR MORDRED WERE BUSY UPON SIR GAWAINE FOR TO DISCLOSE THE LOVE BETWEEN SIR LANCELOT AND QUEEN GUENEVER

IN May when every lusty heart flourisheth and bourgeoneth, for as the season is lusty to behold and comfortable, so man and woman rejoice and gladden of summer coming with his fresh flowers : for winter with his rough winds and blasts causeth a lusty man and woman to cower, and sit fast by the fire. So in this season, as in the month of May, it befell a great anger and unhap that stinted not till the flower of chivalry of all the world was destroyed and slain ; and all was long upon two unhappy knights, the which were named Agravaine and Sir Mordred, that were brethren unto Sir Gawaine.   For this Sir Agravaine and Sir Mordred had ever a privy hate unto the queen Dame Guenever and to Sir Lancelot, and daily and nightly they ever watched upon Sir Lancelot.   So it mishapped, Sir Gawaine and all his brethren

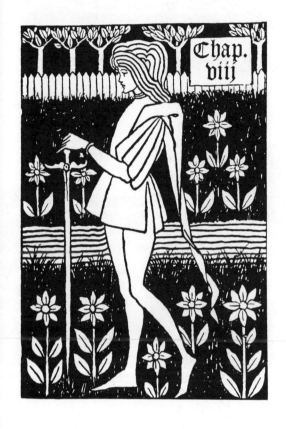

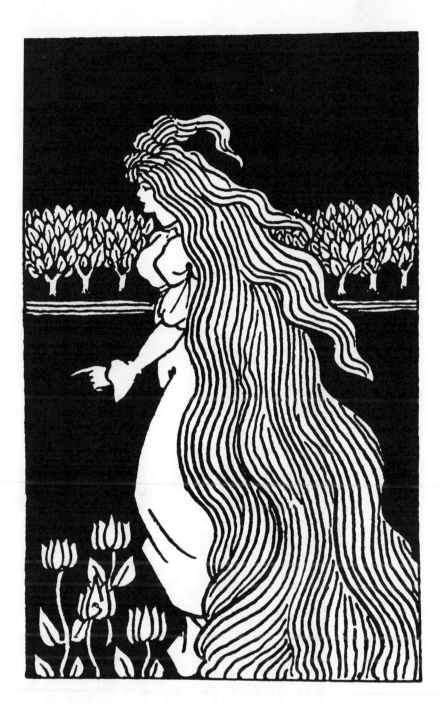

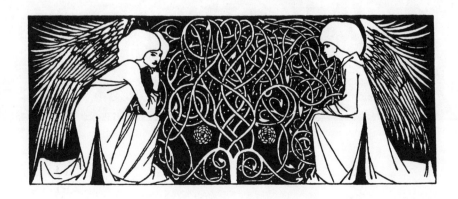

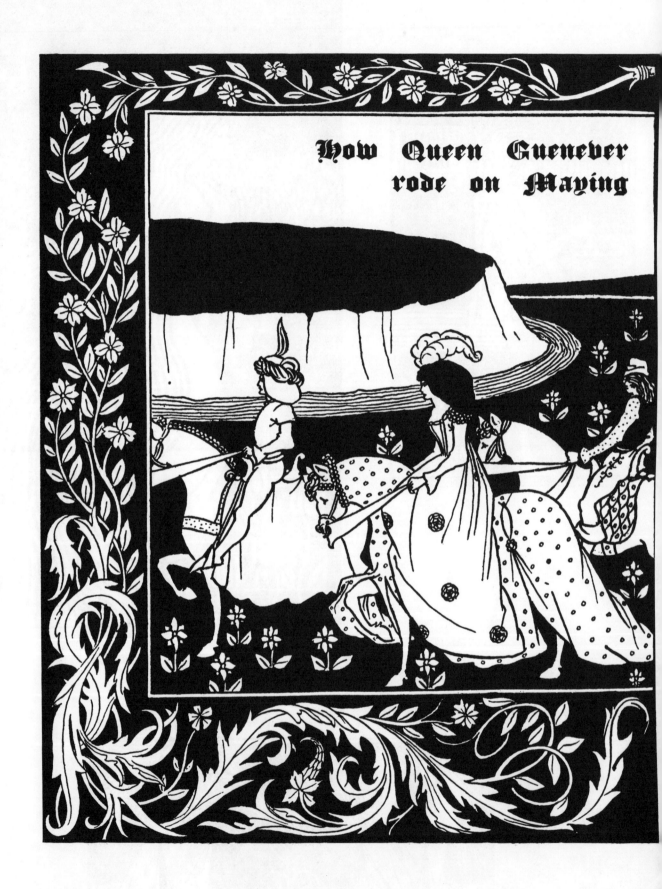

How Queen Guenever rode on Maying

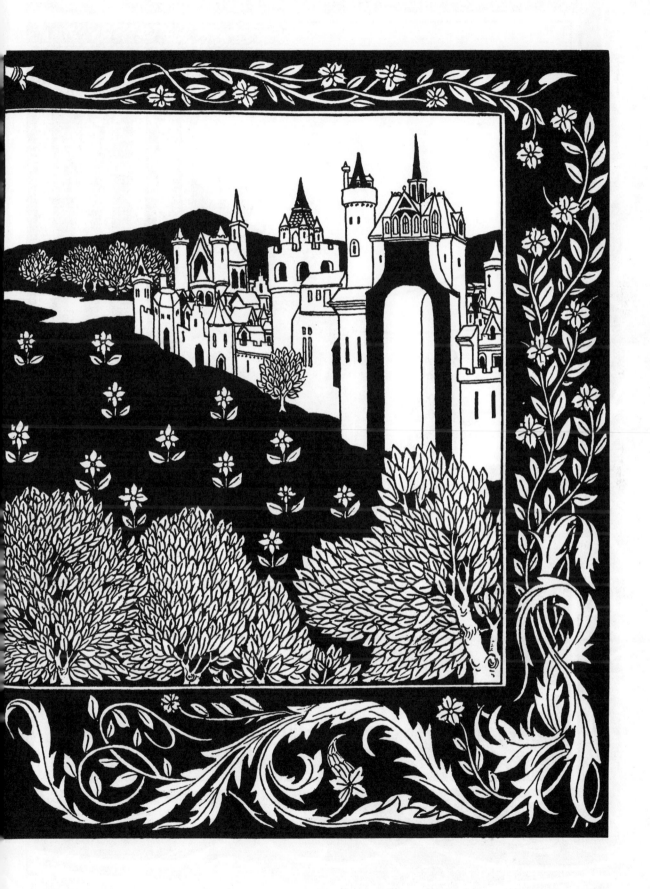

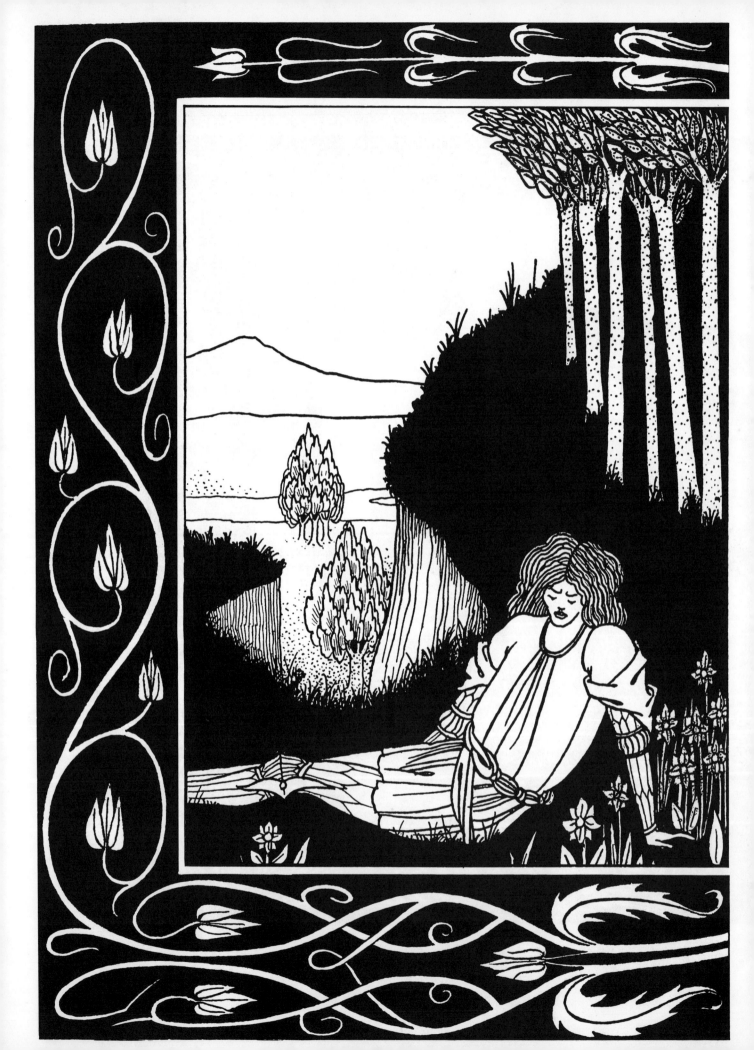

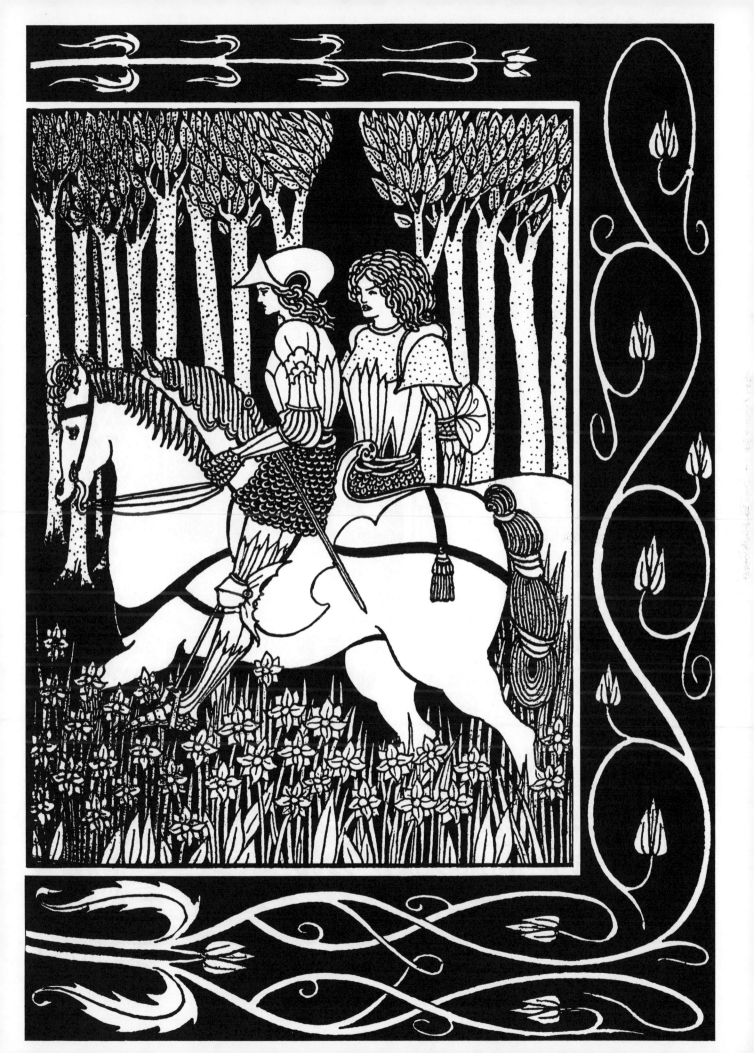

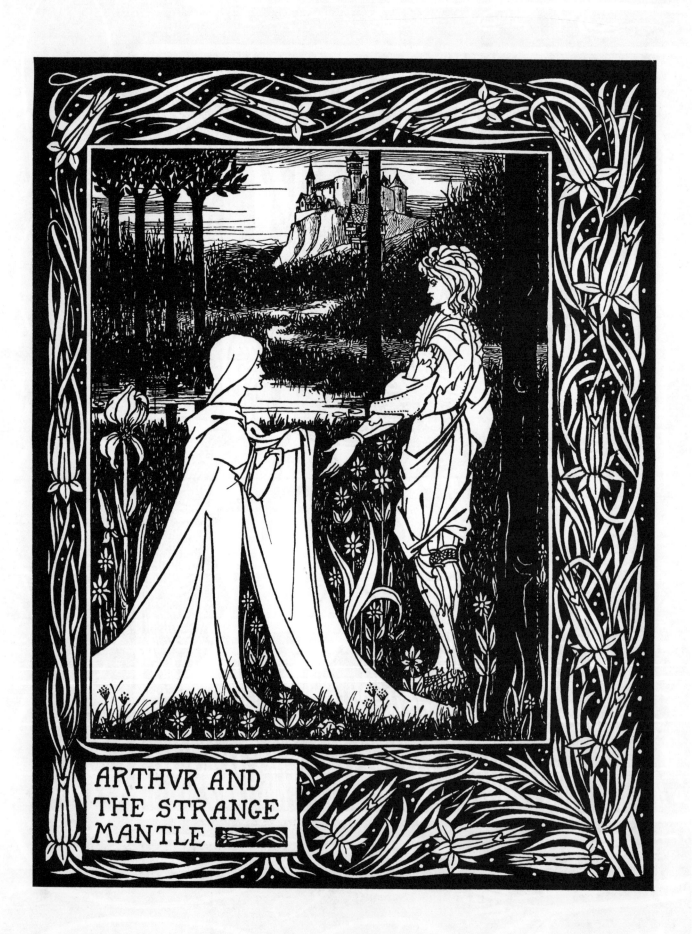

ARTHVR AND
THE STRANGE
MANTLE

Book viij   Chapter j

HOW SIR TRISTRAM DE LIONES WAS BORN, AND HOW
HIS MOTHER DIED AT HIS BIRTH, WHEREFORE SHE
NAMED HIM TRISTRAM.

T was a king that hight Meliodas, and
he was lord and king of the country
of Liones, and this Meliodas was a
likely knight as any was that time
living. And by fortune he wedded
King Mark's sister of Cornwall; and
she was called Elizabeth, that was
called both good and fair. And at
that time King Arthur reigned, and he
was whole king of England, Wales,
and Scotland, and of many other
realms: howbeit there were many
kings that were lords of many countries,
but all they held their lands of King
Arthur; for in Wales were two kings,
and in the north were many kings;
and in Cornwall and in the west were
two kings; also in Ireland were two
or three kings, and all were under
the obeissance of King Arthur. So
was the King of France, and the King of Brittany, and all the
lordships unto Rome. So when this King Meliodas had been
with his wife, within a while she waxed great with child, and
she was a full meek lady, and well she loved her lord, and he
her again, so there was great joy betwixt them. Then there was
a lady in that country that had loved King Meliodas long, and by

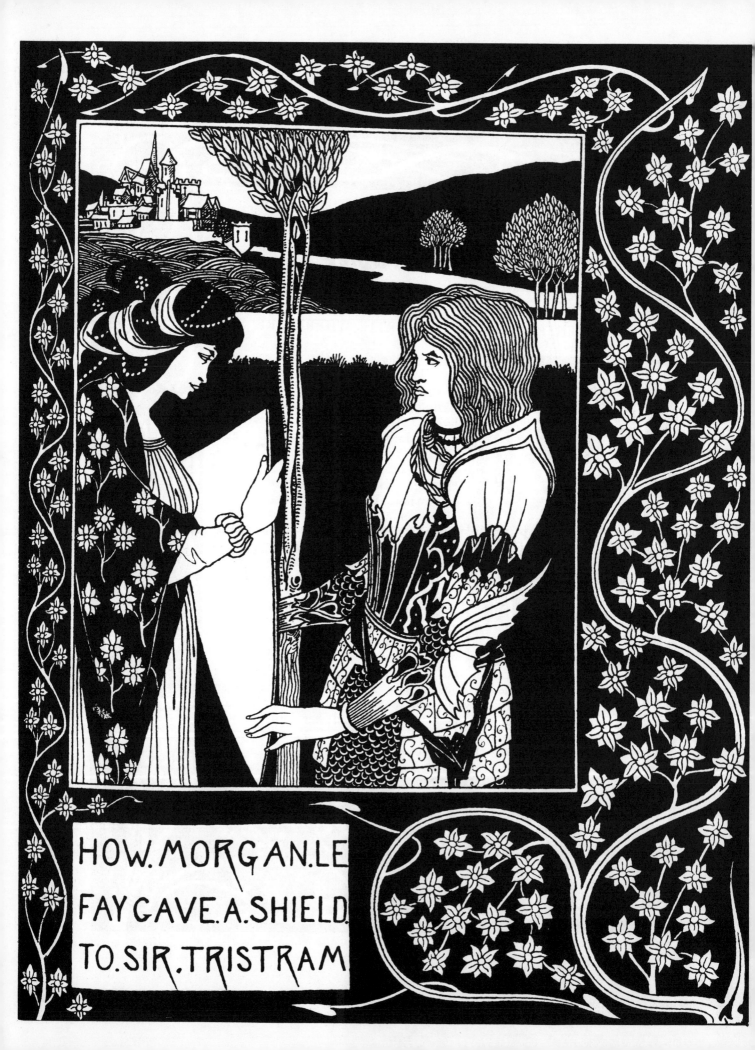

HOW. MORGAN. LE FAY GAVE. A. SHIELD. TO. SIR. TRISTRAM

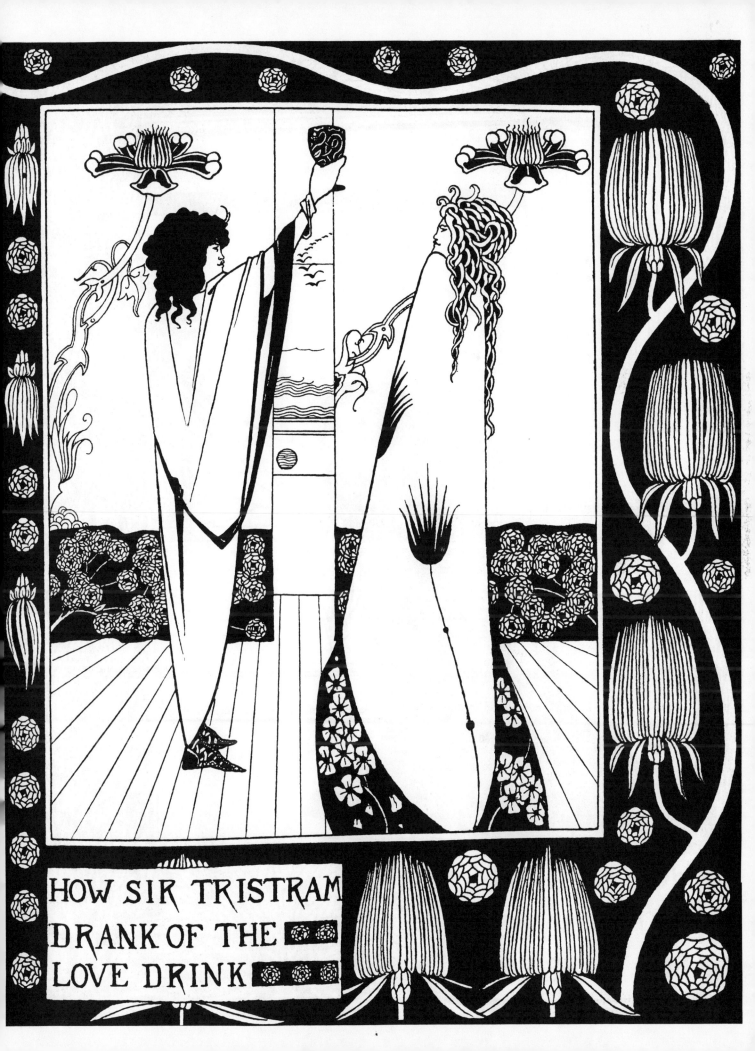

HOW SIR TRISTRAM
DRANK OF THE
LOVE DRINK

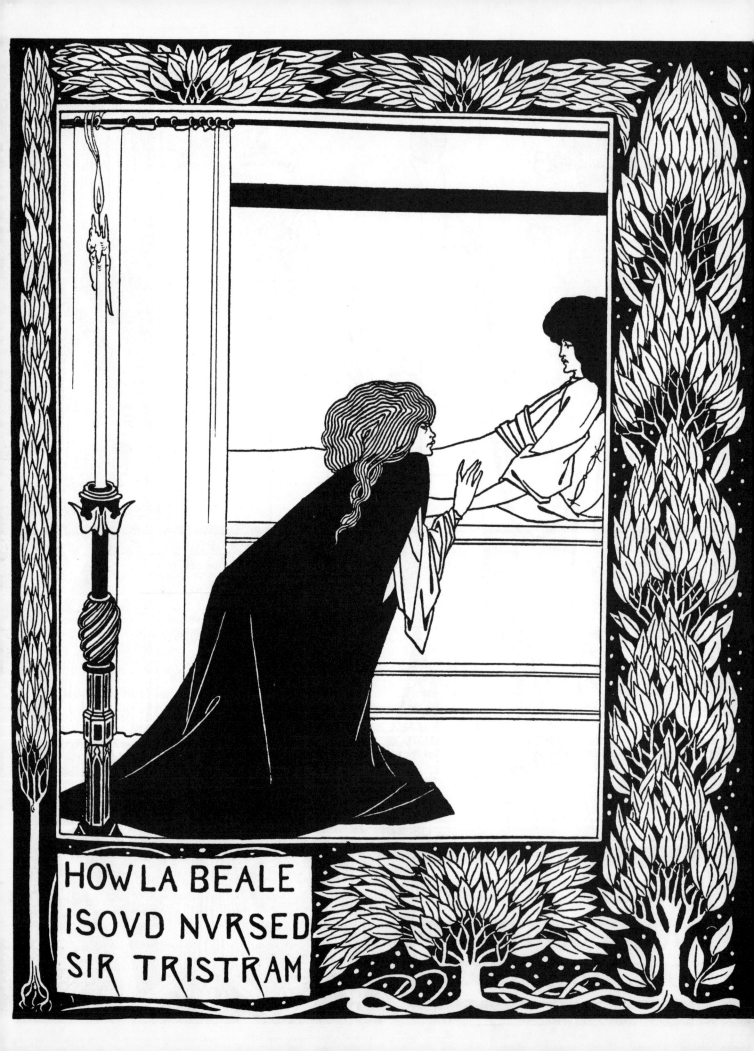

HOW LA BEALE
ISOVD NVRSED
SIR TRISTRAM

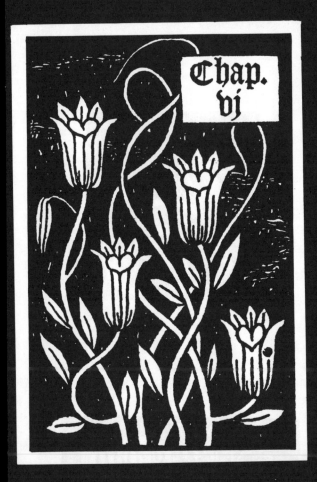

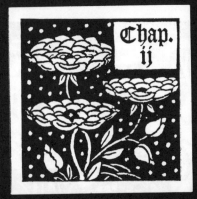

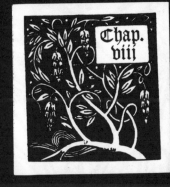

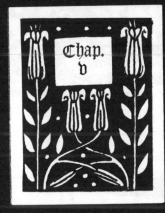

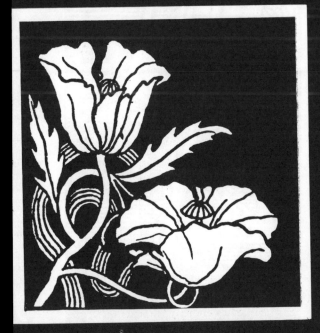

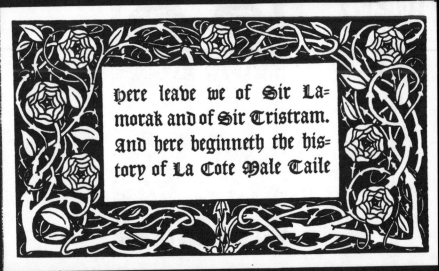

Here leave we of Sir La=
morak and of Sir Tristram.
And here beginneth the his=
tory of La Cote Male Taile

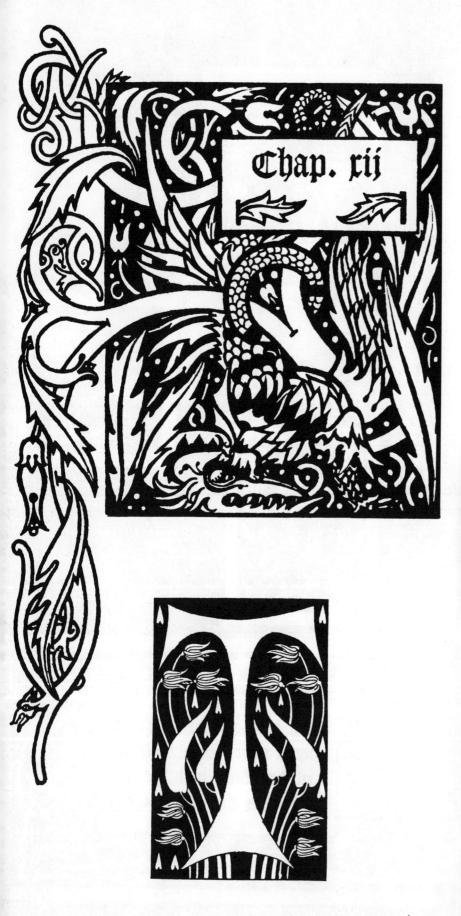

Chap. xij

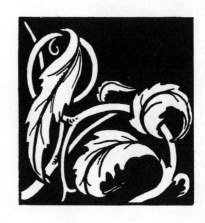

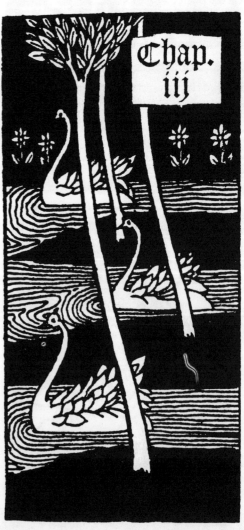

Chap. iij

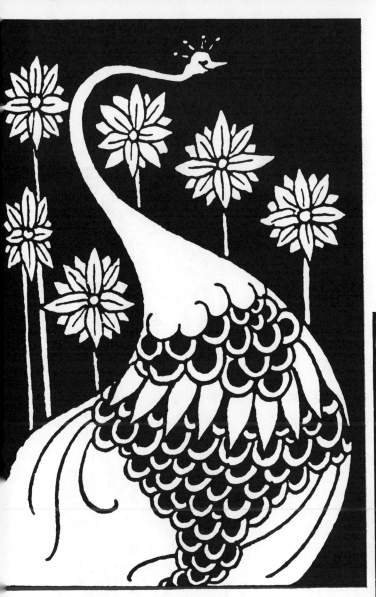

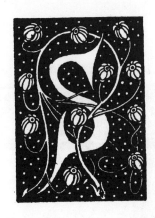

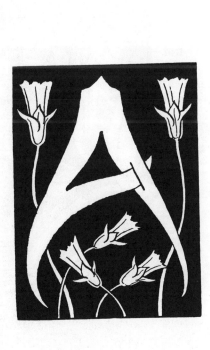

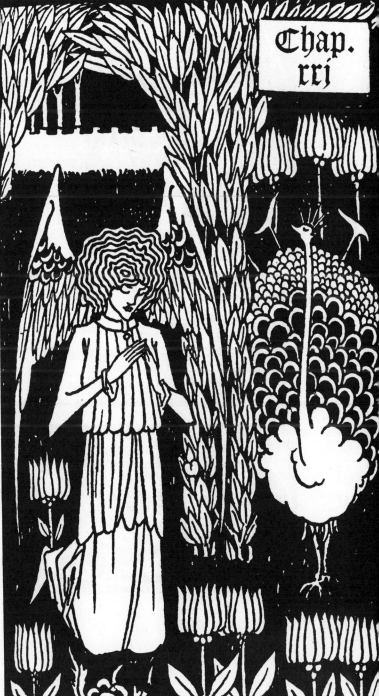

Chap.
rri

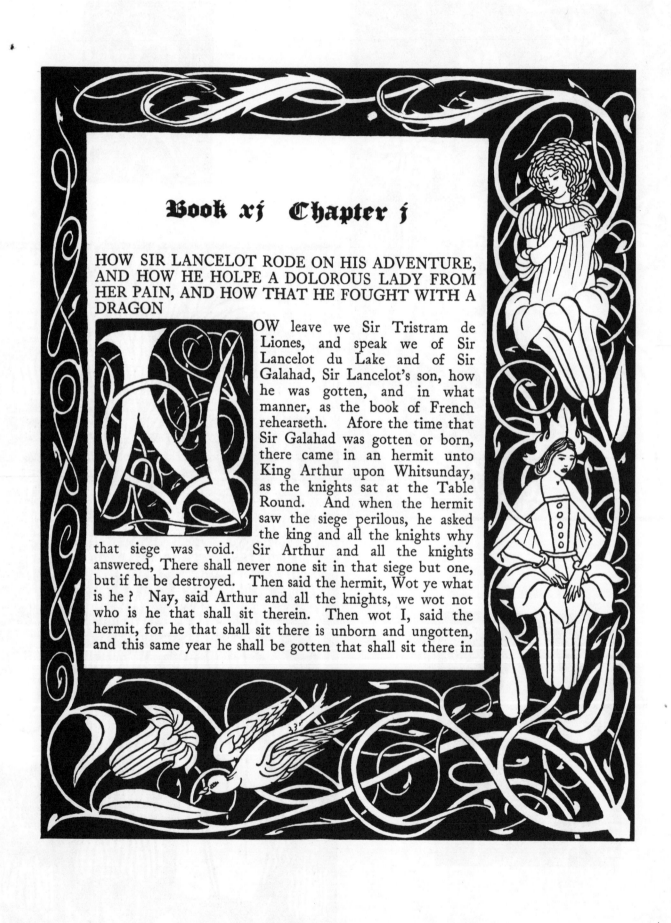

Book xj Chapter j

HOW SIR LANCELOT RODE ON HIS ADVENTURE, AND HOW HE HOLPE A DOLOROUS LADY FROM HER PAIN, AND HOW THAT HE FOUGHT WITH A DRAGON

NOW leave we Sir Tristram de Liones, and speak we of Sir Lancelot du Lake and of Sir Galahad, Sir Lancelot's son, how he was gotten, and in what manner, as the book of French rehearseth. Afore the time that Sir Galahad was gotten or born, there came in an hermit unto King Arthur upon Whitsunday, as the knights sat at the Table Round. And when the hermit saw the siege perilous, he asked the king and all the knights why that siege was void. Sir Arthur and all the knights answered, There shall never none sit in that siege but one, but if he be destroyed. Then said the hermit, Wot ye what is he? Nay, said Arthur and all the knights, we wot not who is he that shall sit therein. Then wot I, said the hermit, for he that shall sit there is unborn and ungotten, and this same year he shall be gotten that shall sit there in

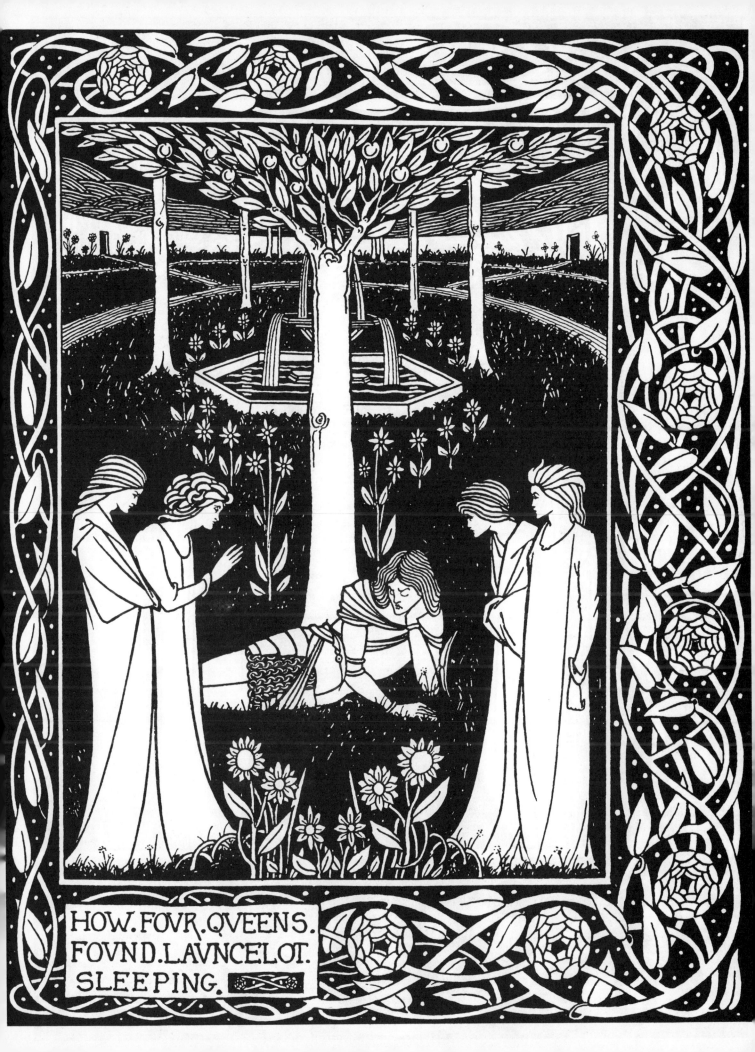

HOW. FOVR. QVEENS.
FOVND. LAVNCELOT.
SLEEPING.

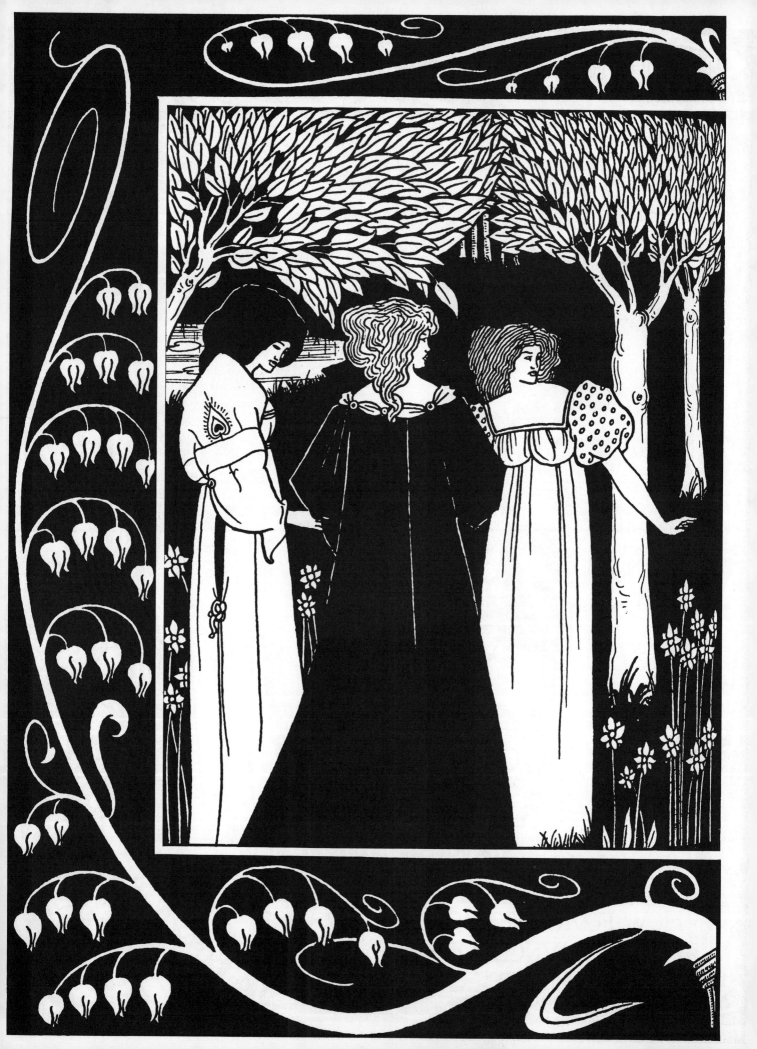

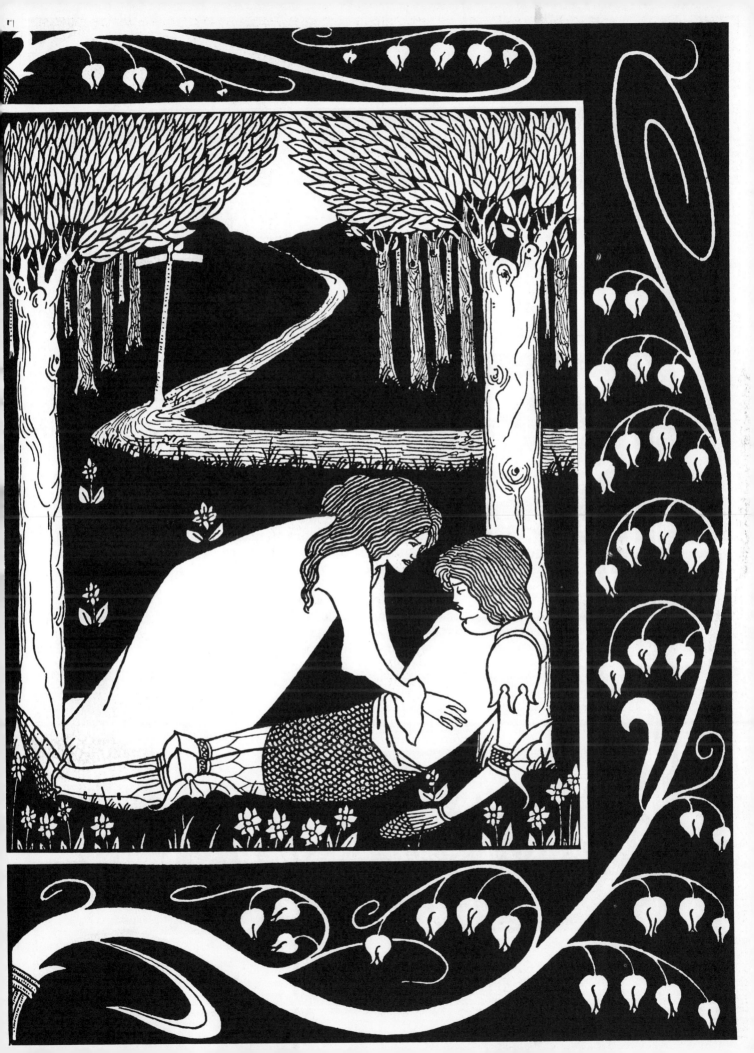

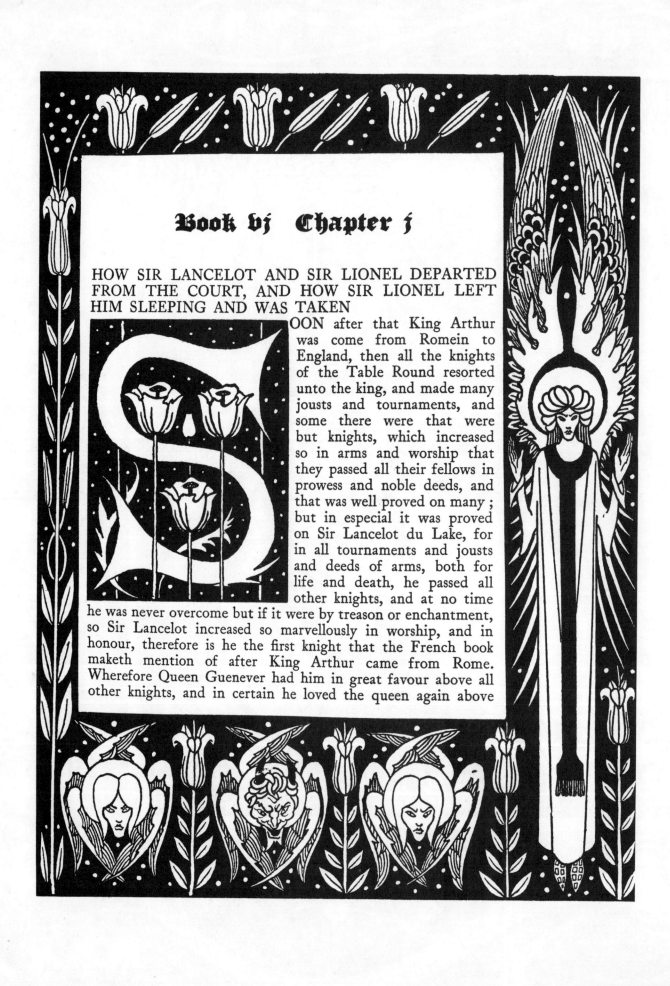

Book vj   Chapter j

HOW SIR LANCELOT AND SIR LIONEL DEPARTED FROM THE COURT, AND HOW SIR LIONEL LEFT HIM SLEEPING AND WAS TAKEN

SOON after that King Arthur was come from Romein to England, then all the knights of the Table Round resorted unto the king, and made many jousts and tournaments, and some there were that were but knights, which increased so in arms and worship that they passed all their fellows in prowess and noble deeds, and that was well proved on many ; but in especial it was proved on Sir Lancelot du Lake, for in all tournaments and jousts and deeds of arms, both for life and death, he passed all other knights, and at no time he was never overcome but if it were by treason or enchantment, so Sir Lancelot increased so marvellously in worship, and in honour, therefore is he the first knight that the French book maketh mention of after King Arthur came from Rome. Wherefore Queen Guenever had him in great favour above all other knights, and in certain he loved the queen again above

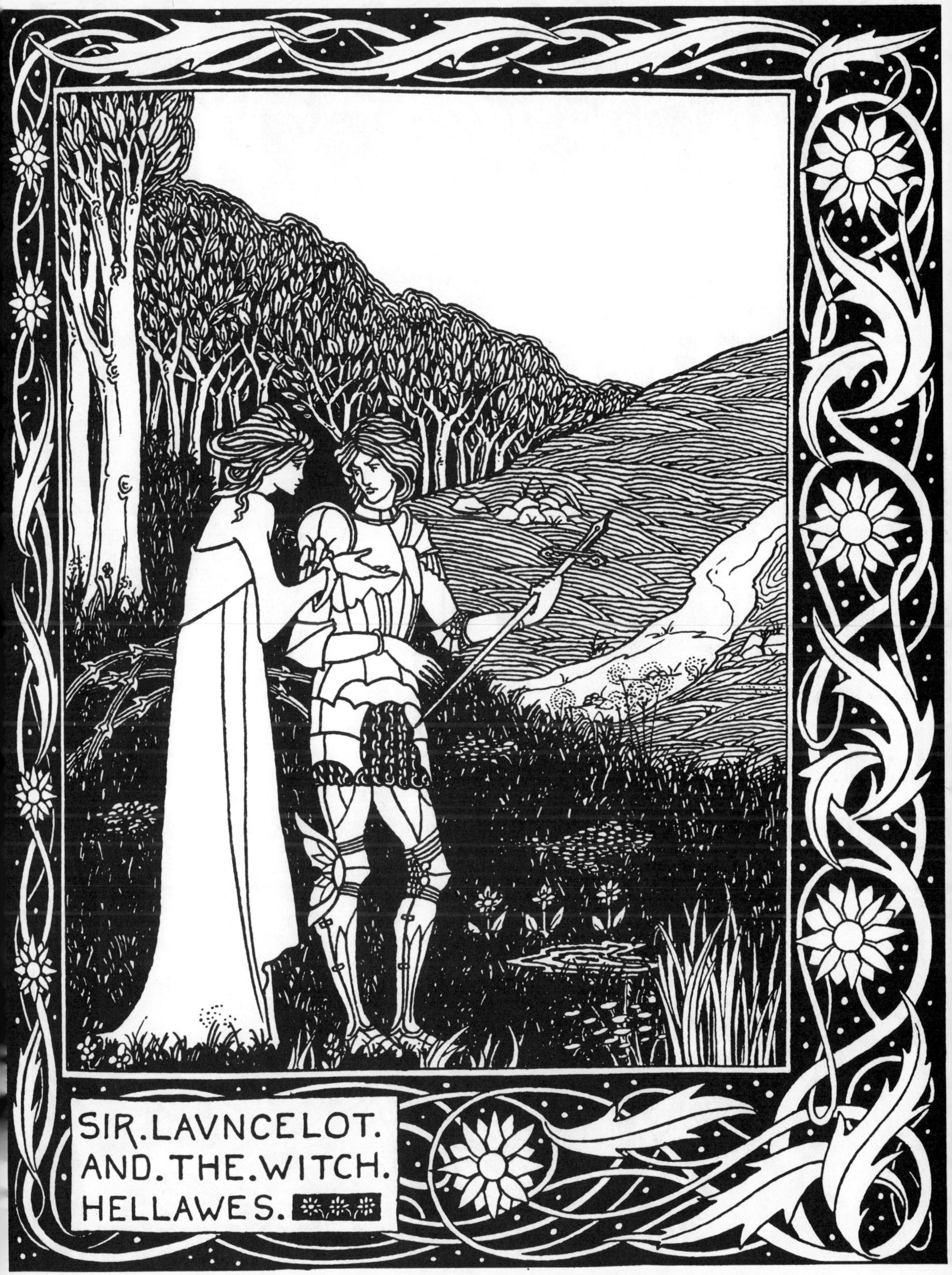

SIR. LAVNCELOT. AND. THE. WITCH. HELLAWES.

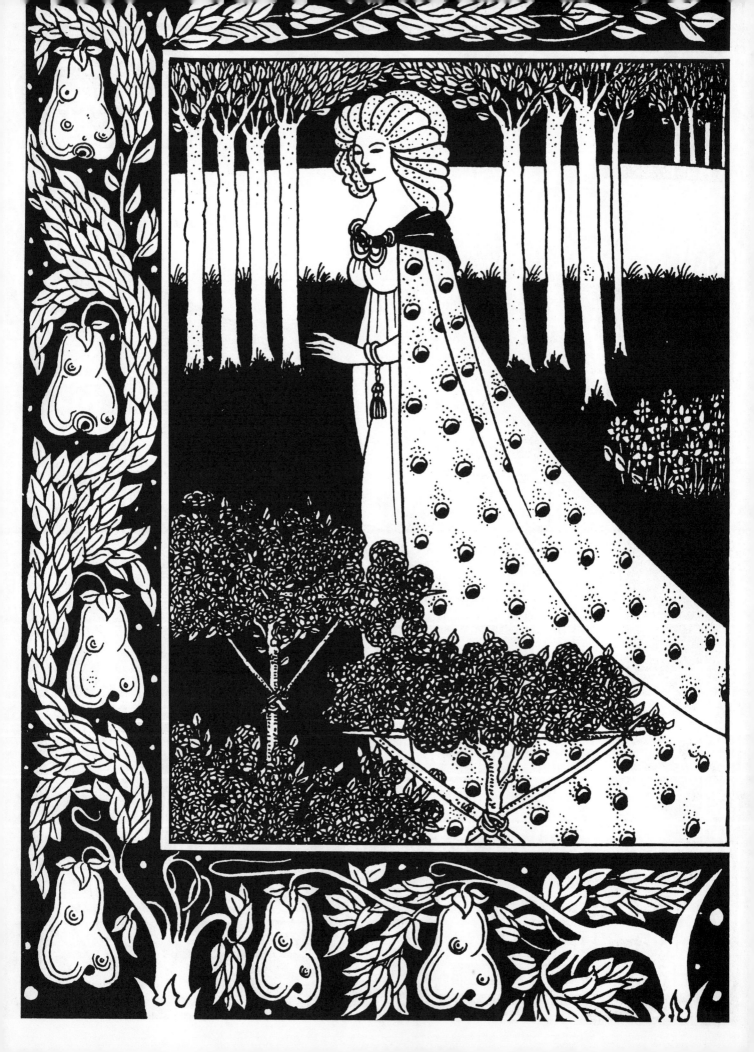

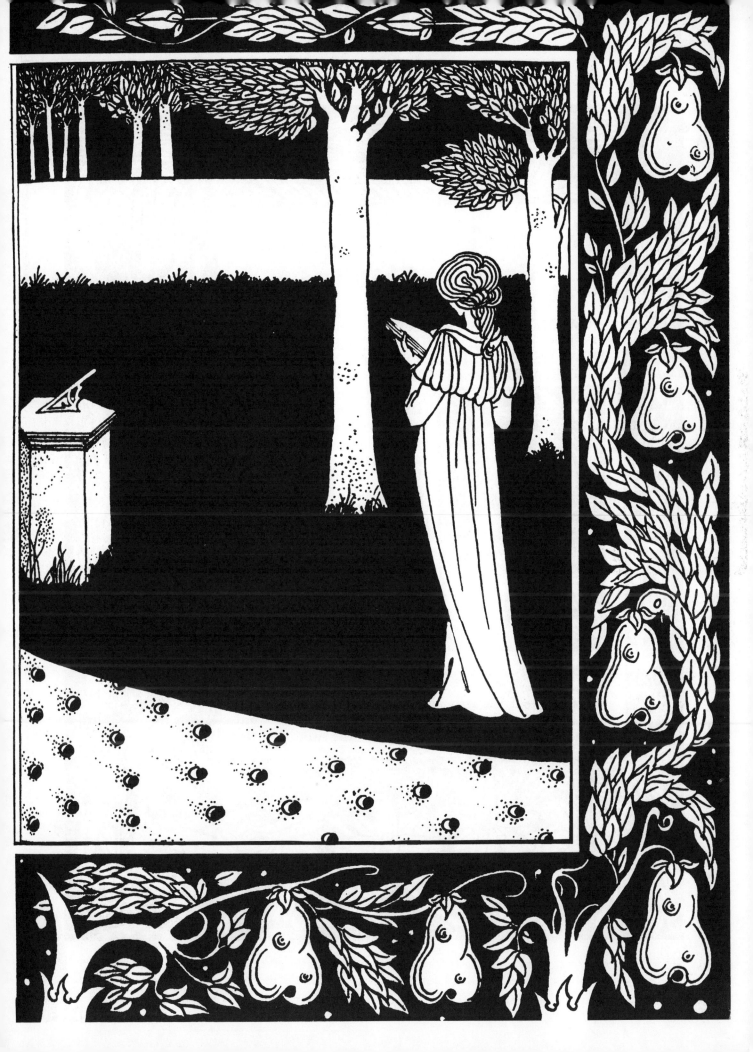

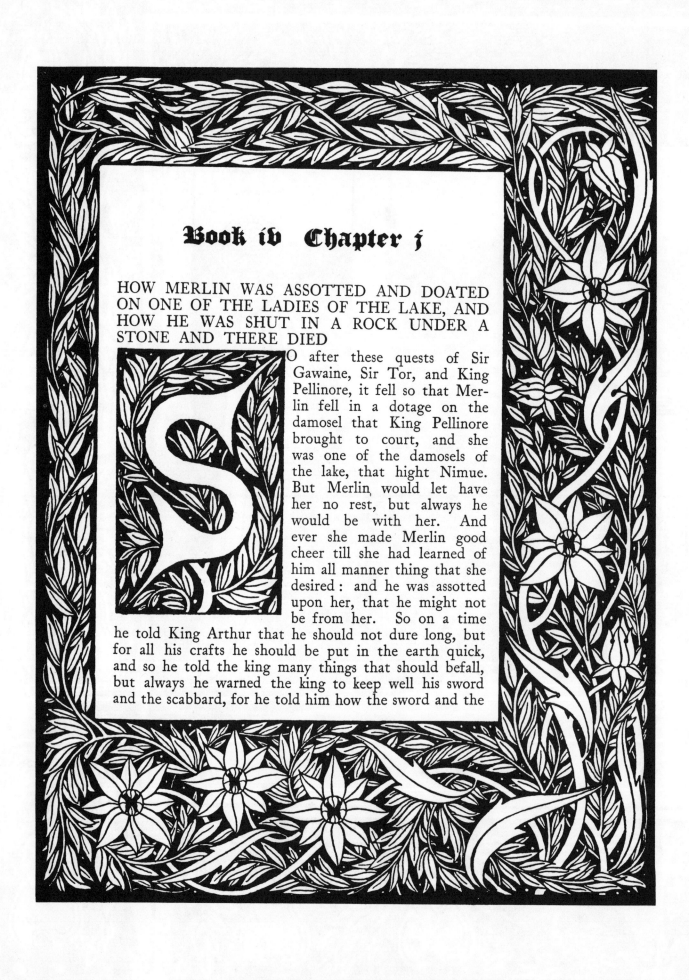

Book iv   Chapter j

HOW MERLIN WAS ASSOTTED AND DOATED
ON ONE OF THE LADIES OF THE LAKE, AND
HOW HE WAS SHUT IN A ROCK UNDER A
STONE AND THERE DIED

SO after these quests of Sir Gawaine, Sir Tor, and King Pellinore, it fell so that Merlin fell in a dotage on the damosel that King Pellinore brought to court, and she was one of the damosels of the lake, that hight Nimue. But Merlin would let have her no rest, but always he would be with her. And ever she made Merlin good cheer till she had learned of him all manner thing that she desired: and he was assotted upon her, that he might not be from her. So on a time he told King Arthur that he should not dure long, but for all his crafts he should be put in the earth quick, and so he told the king many things that should befall, but always he warned the king to keep well his sword and the scabbard, for he told him how the sword and the

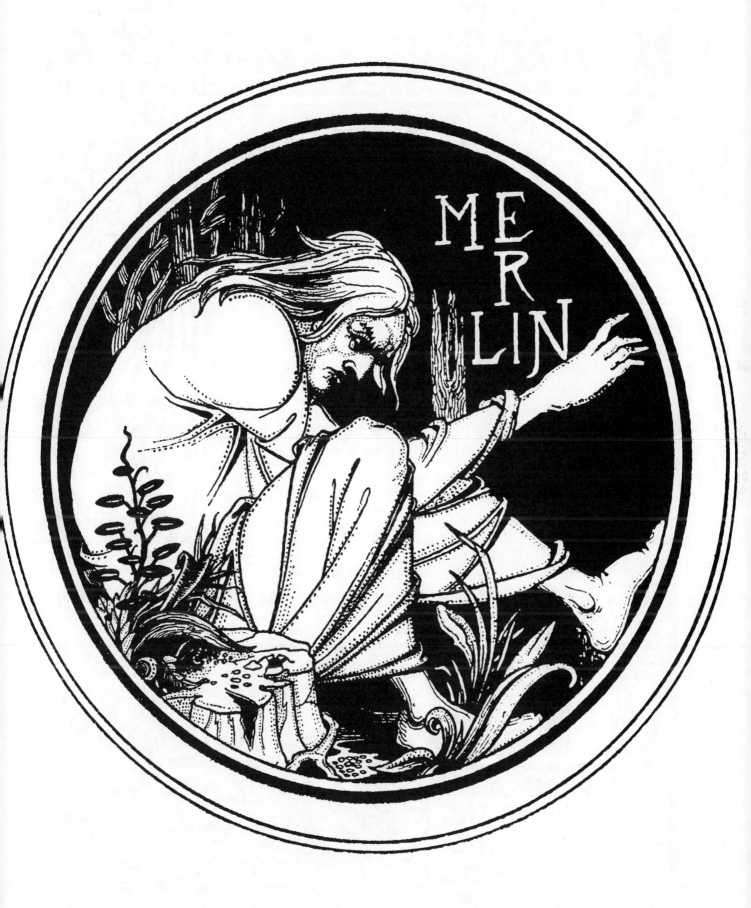

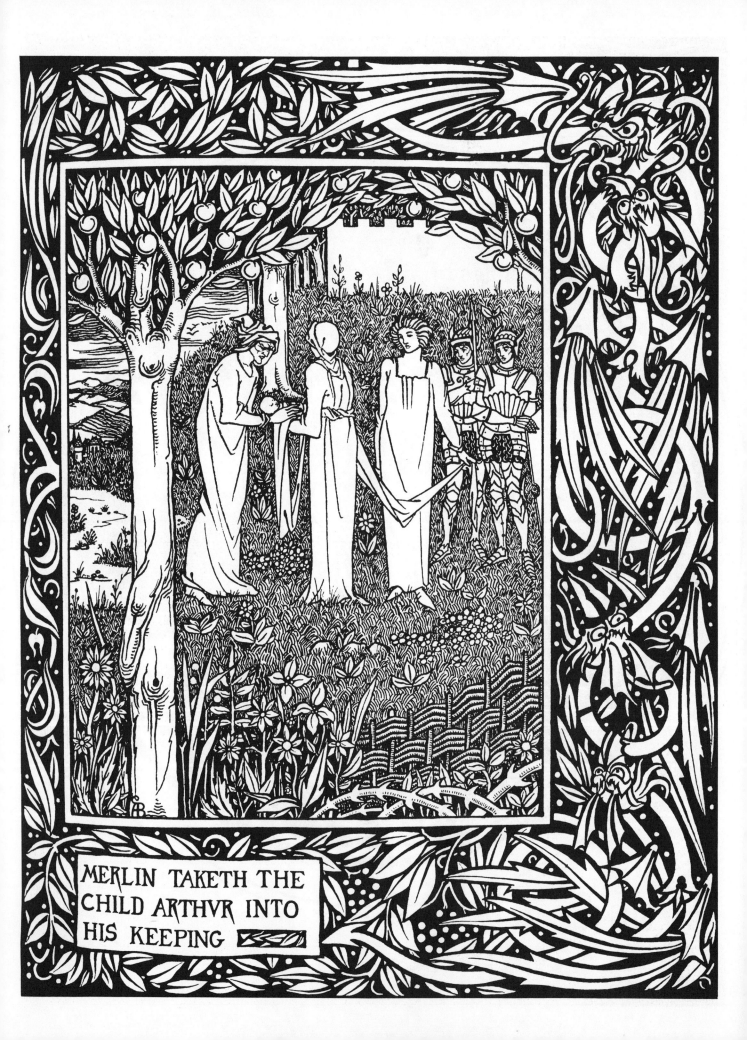

MERLIN TAKETH THE
CHILD ARTHVR INTO
HIS KEEPING

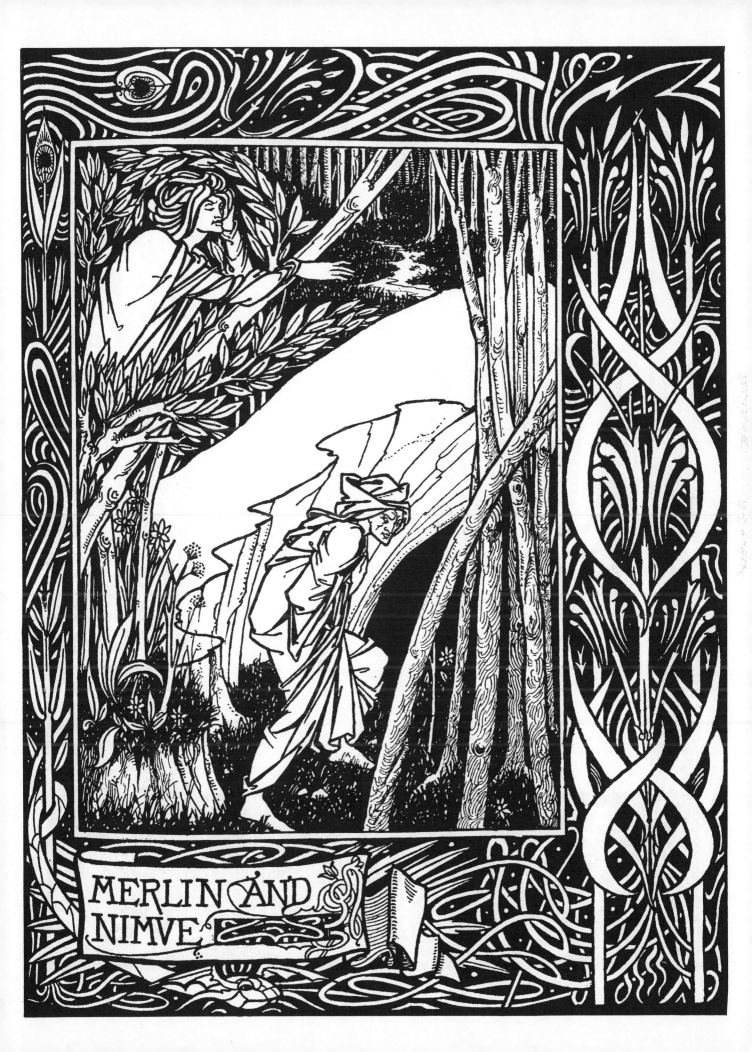

MERLIN AND
NIMVE

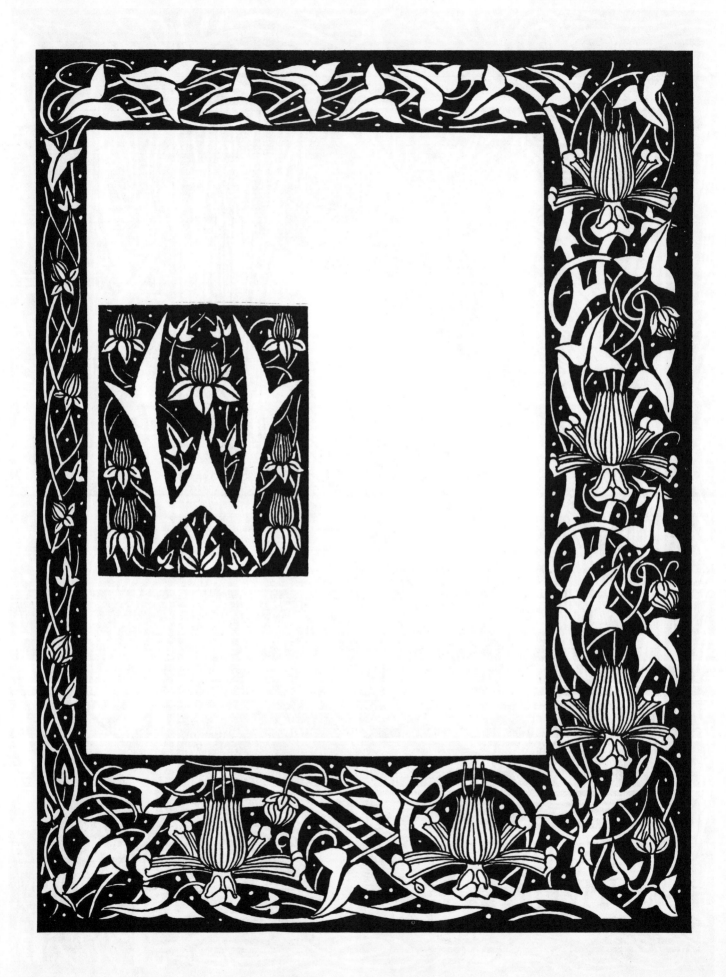

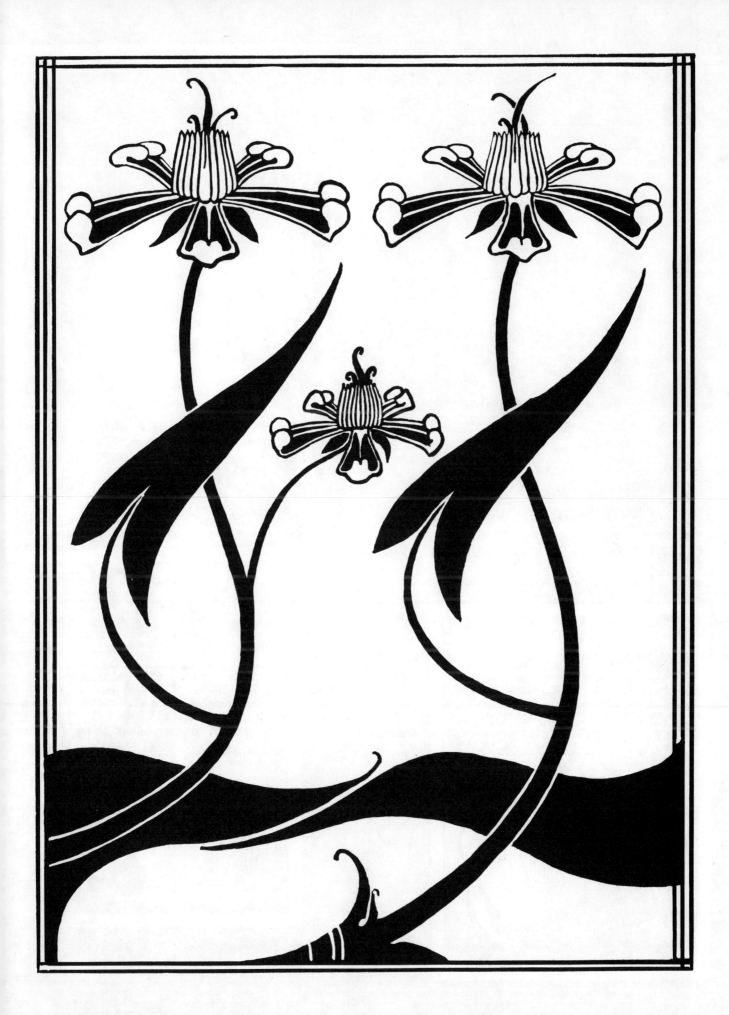

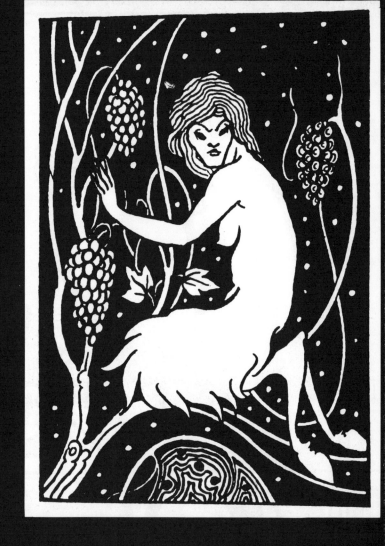

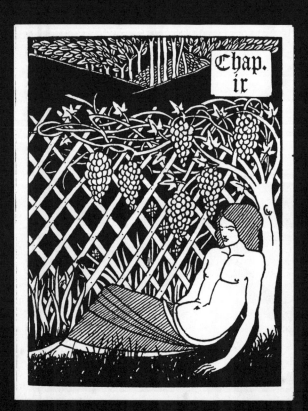

Chap.
ir

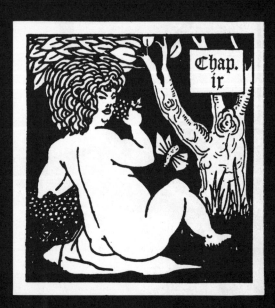

Chap.
ir

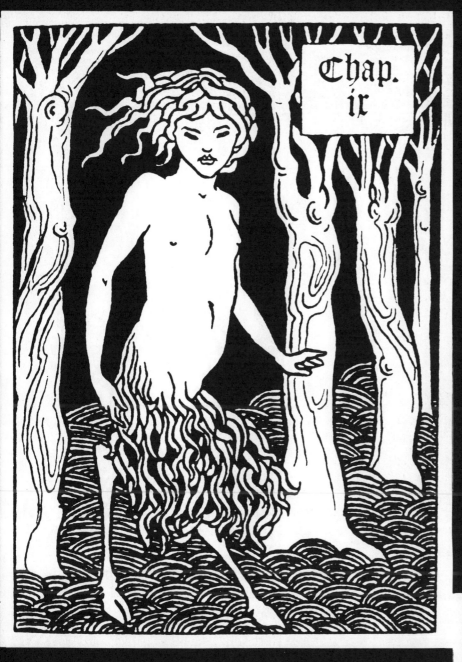

Chap.
ir

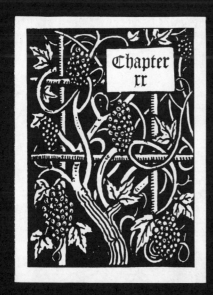

Chapter
rr

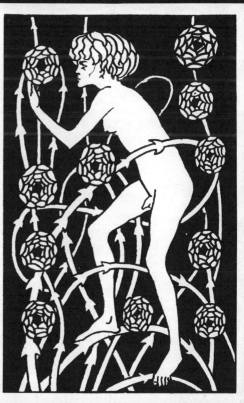

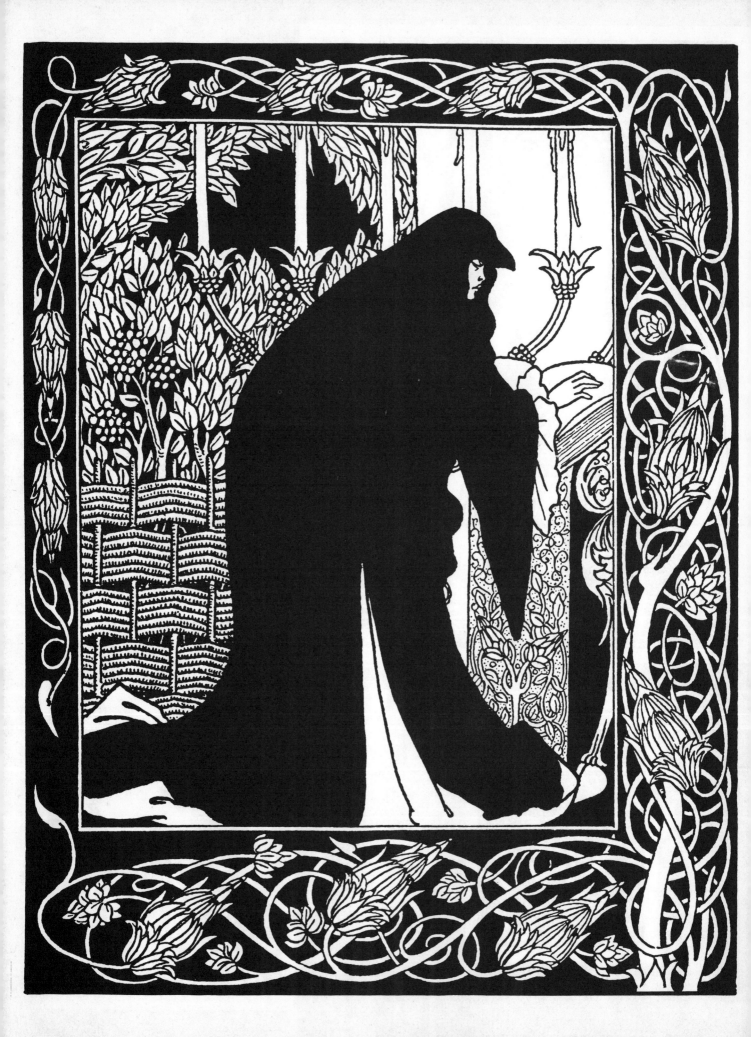

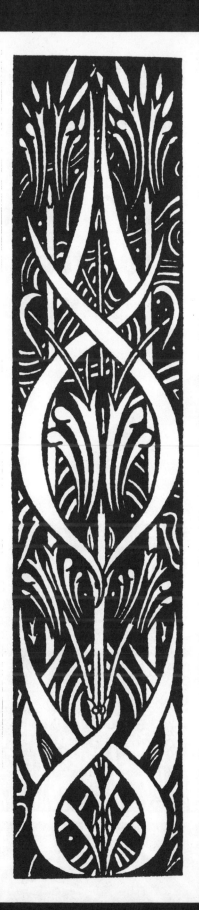

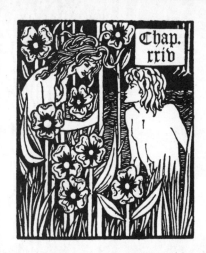

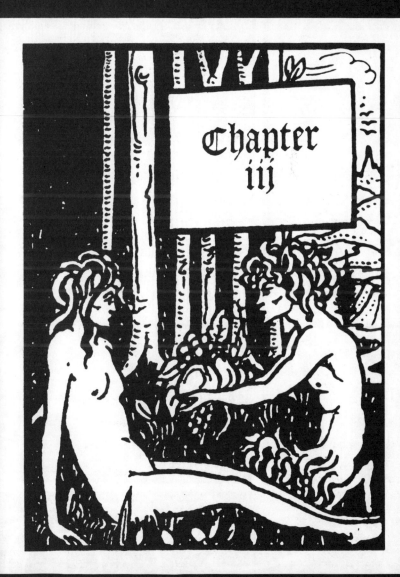

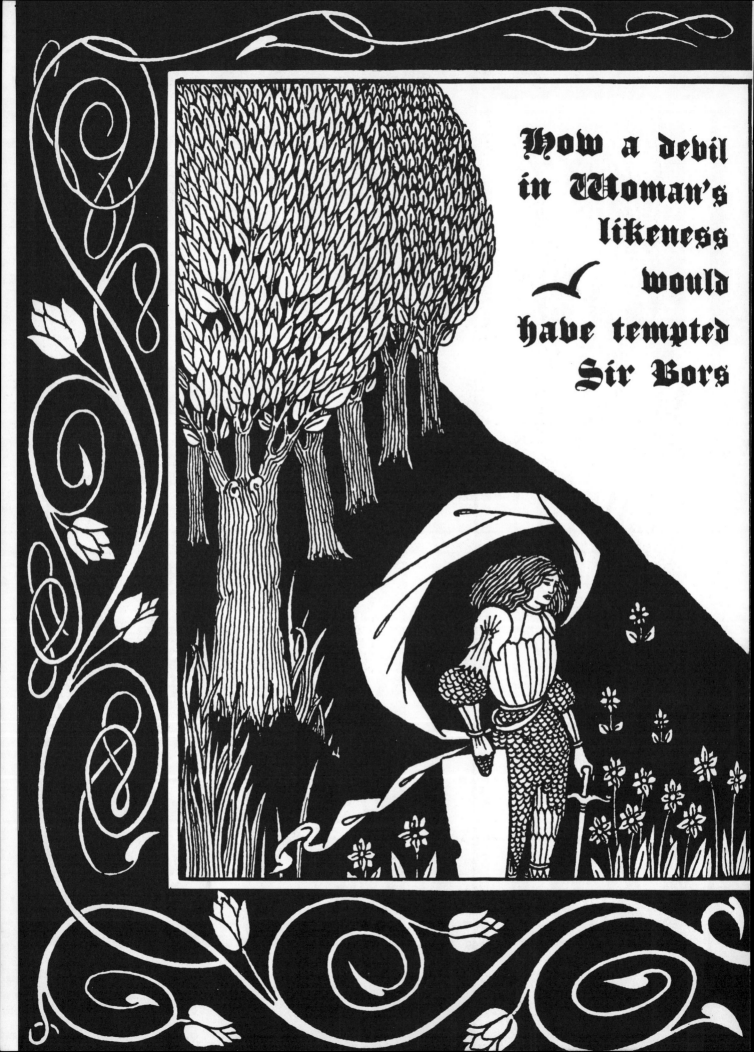

How a devil in Woman's likeness would have tempted Sir Bors

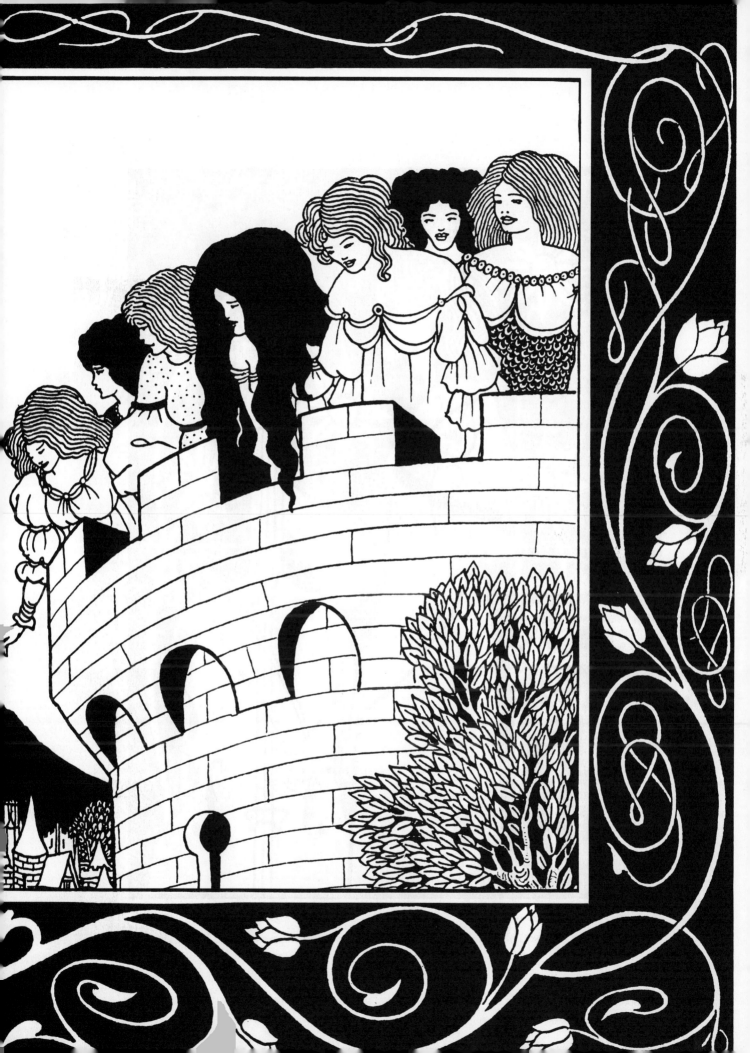

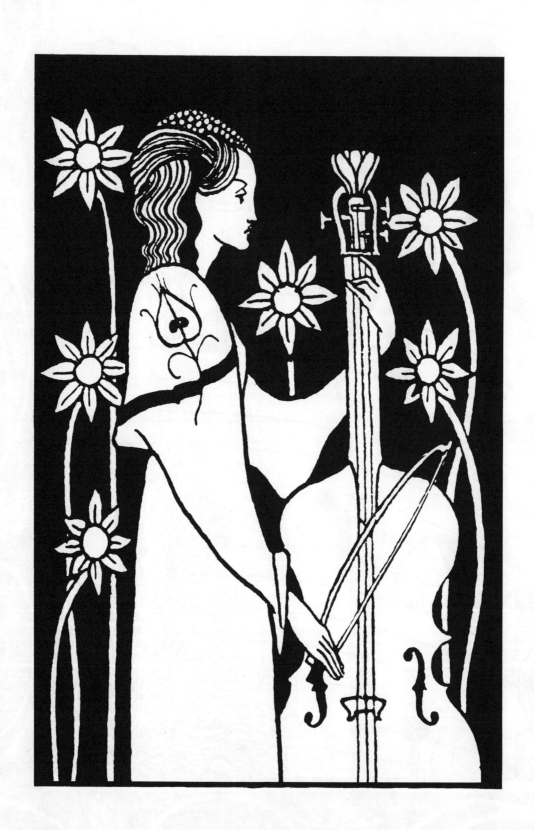

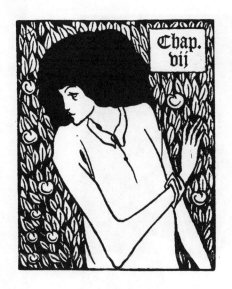

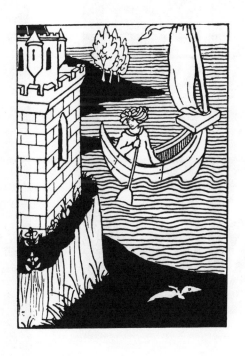

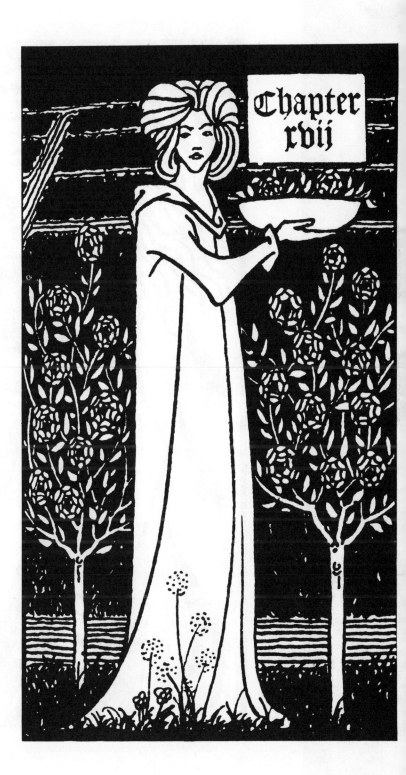

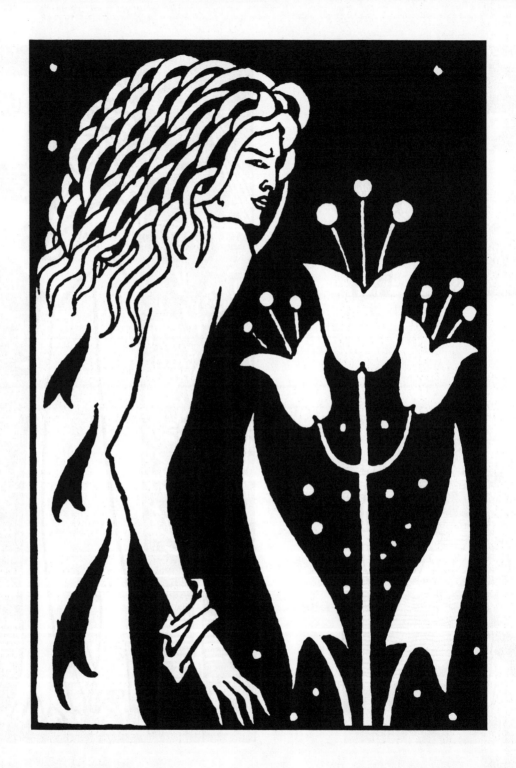

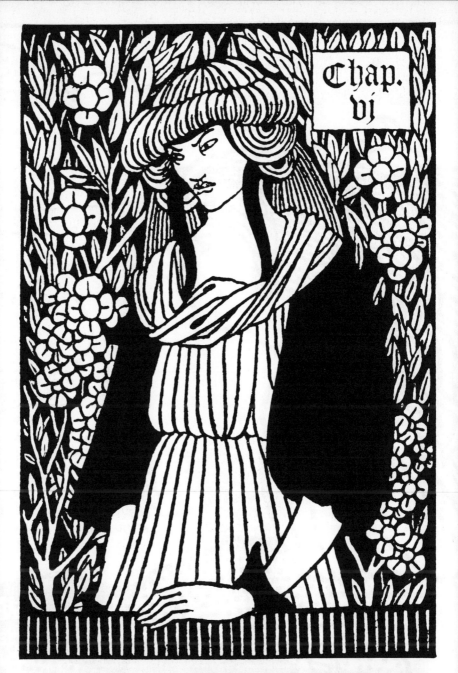

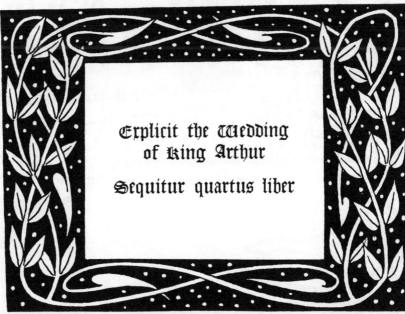

Explicit the Wedding
of King Arthur

Sequitur quartus liber

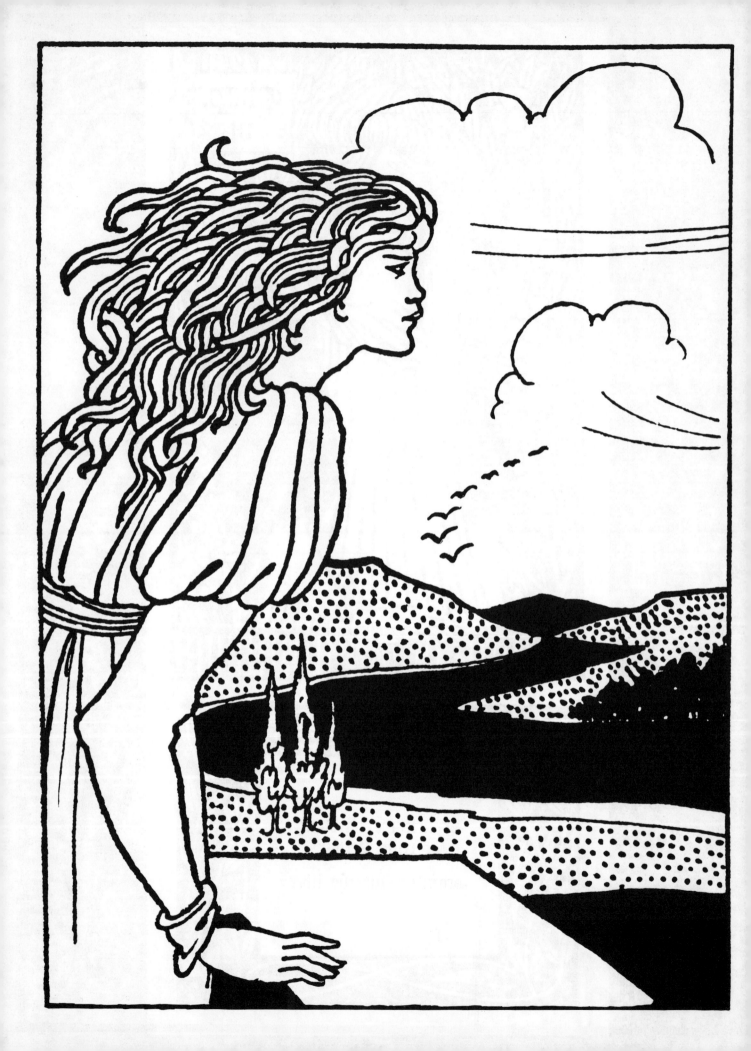

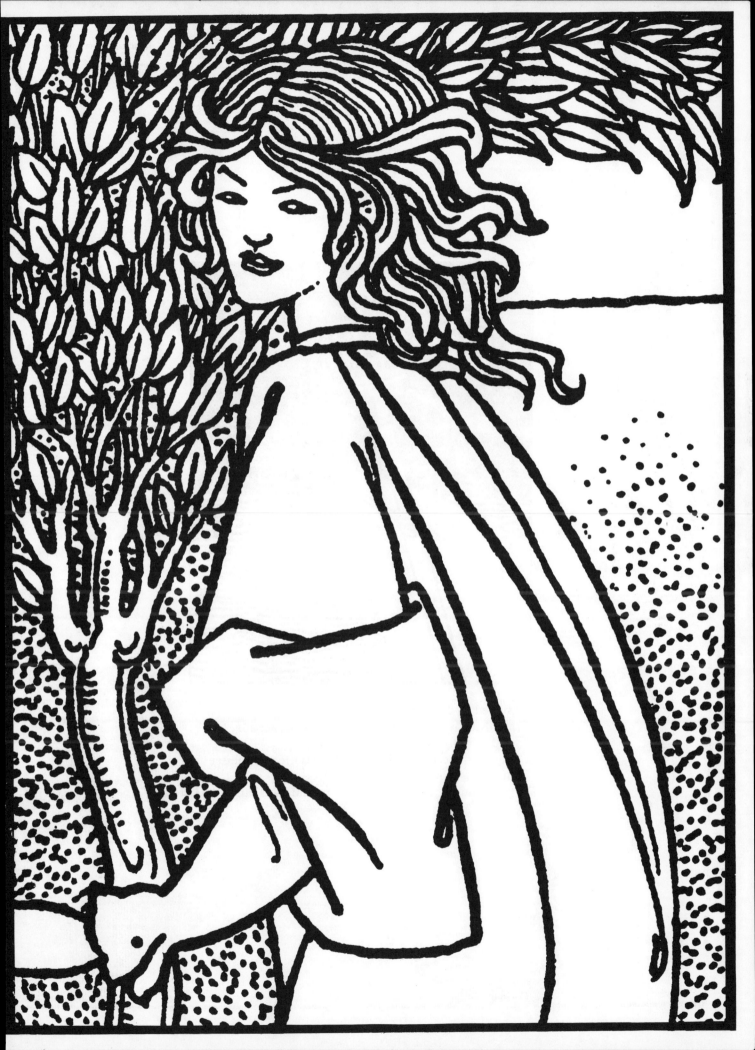

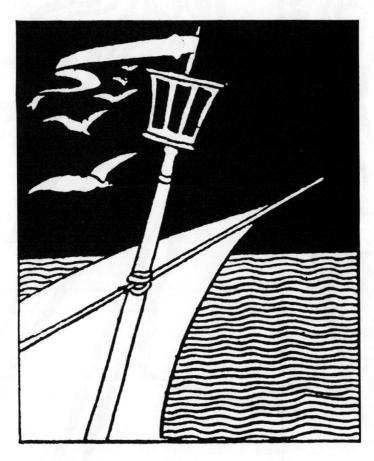

Designed by Barbara Holdridge
Composed by the Service Composition Company,
    Baltimore, Maryland
Covers printed by Rugby, Inc., Knoxville, Tennessee
Printed and bound by Port City Press, Inc.,
    Baltimore, Maryland, on 60-pound Williamsburg Offset